WHAT'S BEYOND?
SOLVING MYSTERIES IN SPACE

MICHAEL CUSACK

SCHOLASTIC INC.
New York Toronto London Auckland Sydney Tokyo

Photo Credits

Cover: Hale Observatories/Frederic Lewis, Inc.
Pp. viii, 7, Smithsonian Institution; pp. 2, 28, American Museum of Natural History; pp. 8, 17, 24, 36, 42, 46, 51, 53, 56, 62, 66, NASA; pp. 12, 72, 88, Hale Observatories; p. 15, Mount Wilson Observatory; pp. 20, 32, 40, Wide World Photos; pp. 60, 81, UPI; p. 68, McDonald Observatory; pp. 76-77, Mount Wilson and Palomar Observatories; p. 86, Lois Cohen, Griffith Observatory; p. 91, Kitt Peak National Observatory; p. 94, California Institute of Technology.

ISBN 0-590-32739-9

Published by Scholastic Inc.

12 11 10 9 8 7 6 5 4 3 2 1 1 4 5 6 7 8/8

Printed in the U.S.A. 01

This book is dedicated to all those who have ever looked at the starry sky and wondered.

Contents

WHAT'S BEYOND?
SOLVING MYSTERIES IN SPACE

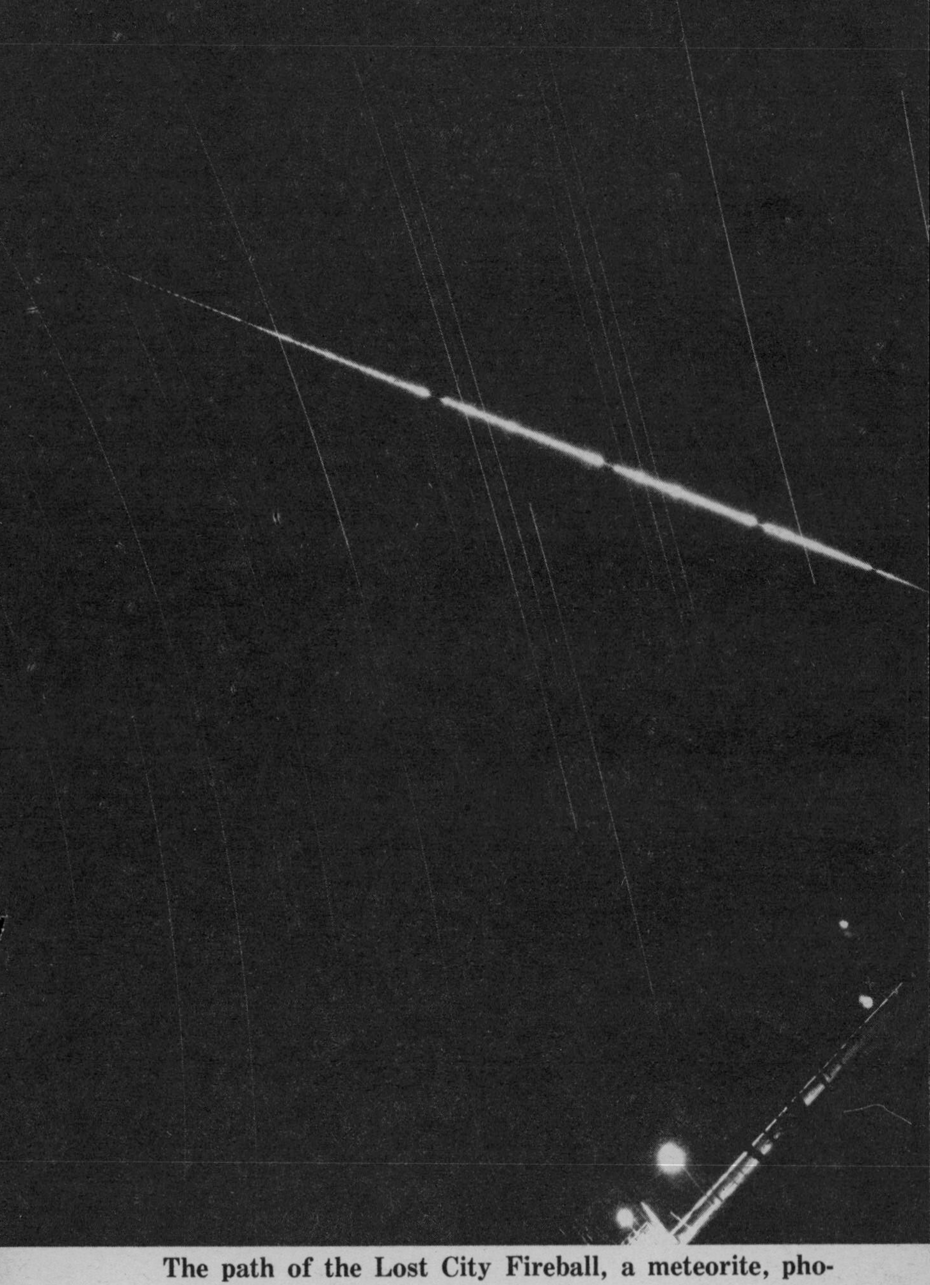

The path of the Lost City Fireball, a meteorite, photographed by automatic cameras.

Meteorites: Space Invaders

Earth is being invaded from space!

It's happening all the time.

Sometimes you can see the invaders coming toward Earth as fiery sparks streaking across the sky. Most people call these space invaders "shooting stars." Scientists call them *meteors*.

Meteors are pieces of rock or metal. As they pass through Earth's atmosphere, these chunks of space matter become white hot and glow in the night sky.

On any given day, thousands of meteors speed into our atmosphere. At certain times of the year, great showers of these objects whiz into our atmosphere. Most of these chunks of space matter are not much bigger than grains of sand. But some can measure miles across. They are going so fast that most of them burn up long before they can reach Earth's surface.

One of the largest iron meteorites found on Earth is moved into the American Museum of Natural History in New York City in 1897. You can see it now in the museum's Hall of Meteorites and Minerals.

Crashing Through

A chunk of matter whizzing through space outside Earth's atmosphere is called a *meteoroid.* If it enters the atmosphere and is seen as a fiery streak in the sky, it is called a *meteor.* If any of it survives to reach Earth's surface, it's called a *meteorite*.

About twenty fairly large meteorites reach Earth's surface each year. Some fall into oceans or remote places where they can't be recovered. Some are rounded up by scientists. The best of these usually end up in museums.

There are three basic types of meteorites: iron, stony-iron, and stony. Iron meteorites are almost pure metal. They are rich in iron with small amounts of nickel and other metals.

Iron meteorites usually don't look like the Earth rocks around them. Even ones that have been on Earth for thousands of years are fairly easy to spot. An iron meteorite is usually much heavier than an Earth rock of the same size, and its surface often shows signs of having melted. It also tends to be scarred and blackened from its fiery trip through the atmosphere.

Stony and stony-iron meteorites that have been on Earth for some time resemble the surrounding rocks. Wind and rain wear away the blackened crust until the meteorite eventually looks a lot like an Earth rock. Some scientists say that a great many stony and stony-iron meteorites may be lying around on Earth unrecognized. Perhaps that's why most large meteorites in museums are the iron type. But another reason may be that iron meteorites are less likely to break up in the atmosphere.

Most of the stony and stony-iron meteorites in museums were found shortly after they were seen falling to Earth. Chance and luck usually play a big part in these discoveries.

About fifteen years ago, several scientists in the United States decided to give luck a helping hand. They began a network of tracking stations to photograph meteors. By studying the photographs, it was thought they could track the path of a meteor to Earth, and perhaps even trace its path back to deep space.

The Lost City Fireball

One of the best known meteor tracking networks is called the Prairie Network in the United States' Midwest. It's operated by the Smithsonian Institution. Each station in the network has four cameras scanning different sections of the sky. Each evening, the cameras are automatically turned on in the hope of "catching" a meteor.

The cameras were on in the early evening of January 3, 1970, when a very bright light was seen in the sky over Oklahoma. One scientist who saw the light said it was a *bolide*. That's the scientific name for a very bright meteor. Most people call this type of flaming meteor a "fireball."

Dr. Gunther Schwartz, the scientist in charge of the Prairie Network, heard about the Oklahoma fireball on the evening news. He was at home in

Lincoln, Nebraska, at the time. He called network employees in Oklahoma and Kansas to check the cameras in the tracking stations there.

Dr. Schwartz hoped that at least one of the tracking stations had photographed the huge meteor. He also hoped that part of the great fireball had survived to reach Earth. That seemed too much to wish for, but Dr. Schwartz was in luck. An Oklahoma tracking station had photographed the meteor. Information from the photos was fed into a computer, and soon the Smithsonian scientists had a clear idea of the meteor's path. It seemed to come from a region in space beyond the planet Mars. And it seemed to go to a point on Earth near Lost City, Oklahoma.

Dr. Schwartz drove to Lost City. If any piece of the fireball had survived to reach Earth, he was going to find it. After a night's rest in Lost City, Dr. Schwartz drove out into the country to ask farmers whether they had seen the fireball. As he drove along one icy, snow-covered road, Dr. Schwartz suddenly swerved to avoid hitting a strange, black rock no bigger than a football.

What was it doing in the middle of the road? Could it be . . . ?

Dr. Schwartz hopped out of the car and picked up the strange rock. After examining it carefully, Dr. Schwartz felt sure he had a meteorite. Later, lab tests proved he was right. Tracking information on the Lost City Meteorite showed that it had come from an area in space between Mars and Jupiter—the area known as the Asteroid Belt.

Pieces of a Lost Planet?

Thousands of objects travel around the Sun in an area between the planets Jupiter and Mars. The largest of these objects are called asteroids.

Thousands, maybe millions, of chunks of rock and metal make up the Asteroid Belt. Most are tiny. But some measure miles across. Ceres, the largest, is about 440 miles wide.

The larger asteroids are sometimes called "minor planets." They seem to be made up of the same materials as the thousands of other objects in the Asteroid Belt. And all appear to have formed around the same time.

Many people wonder: Where did all these objects come from? Are they pieces of a planet that broke up long, long ago? Or are they the material for a planet that didn't form?

There's a regular pattern in the way the planets of the solar system are spaced. Scientists noticed that pattern a long time ago. They used it to predict the location of the outer planets—Uranus, Neptune, and Pluto—long before those planets were even seen. But there is a gap in the pattern of the planets. Several scientists point out that there is space for another planet between Mars and Jupiter.

This blackened, stony meteorite was called the Lost City Fireball as it streaked across the night sky. **(See photo facing page 1.)**

What's the calculated orbit of that other planet? You guessed it, right where the Asteroid Belt is now.

Did some great explosion rip apart a planet in that region? Or did some object rushing in from

This stony meteorite, found in Antarctica in 1979, may be a piece of Mars. Tests reveal materials in it similar to those on Mars's surface.

deep space collide with a planet that was already there?

Until recently, most scientists believed that the Asteroid Belt held the remnants of a lost planet. Some scientists still believe that. But more and more scientists have come to believe that the Asteroid Belt contains the material for a planet that never had a chance to form.

The Planet That Never Was?

According to one scientific theory, our planet was formed out of a mass of swirling stardust. The great force behind this action was the force of gravity.

Particles of matter in space attract one another. Large particles pull in small ones. This is the force of gravity at work. In time, the swirling stardust might have formed great globs of matter. And this could have led to the formation of our solar system—the Sun, planets, and moons.

Some scientists argue that in order to form a planet, there must be a peaceful setting. Anything that disturbs the neighborhood would prevent chunks of matter from clustering into a planet. This, the scientists say, is what happened in the region between Mars and Jupiter. Jupiter's vast size was likely to have been a disturbing influence on the chunks of matter between Jupiter and Mars. Also, Jupiter seems to give off more energy than it takes in from the Sun. Therefore, the pieces of matter never had a chance to become a planet. The setting was never peaceful enough.

If that's true, then the Asteroid Belt contains some of the stuff our planet was made from. A number of scientists believe that the Asteroid Belt contains *genesis rocks*. These are pieces of material that have remained unchanged since the beginning of our solar system. Since rocks frequently whiz out of the Asteroid Belt toward Earth, isn't it possible that some of them are genesis rocks?

Yes and no!

Studies show that some meteorites are, perhaps, 7 billion years old. That's older than Earth. That may in fact be the age of our solar system. Therefore, these meteorites may have been rocks orbiting the Sun since the birth of our solar system.

But at least two events are likely to have changed these rocks.

Some force was needed to knock such a rock out of the Asteroid Belt in the first place. And that would probably cause a change in the rock. Certainly the rock's fiery trip through the atmosphere would have changed it. Many substances in the original object would burn or break away. Remaining substances would be changed by great heat and contact with chemicals in the atmosphere. Therefore, any meteorite on Earth is likely to be very different from the genesis rocks or other objects traveling in the Asteroid Belt.

Asteroid Hunters

Scientists would like to snare a small asteroid

in space and bring it back to Earth unchanged. But that would not be an easy job. Capturing asteroids in space is probably far in the future. But other space invaders are being captured right now. Almost every week, NASA sends a plane far up into the atmosphere, to around 70,000 feet, to gather dust—asteroid dust, comet dust, and cosmic dust from distant stars. About 10,000 tons of this out-of-this-world dust enters Earth's atmosphere each year. We even breathe in tiny particles of it. It's our everyday link to the stars.

Studies show that most of the dust is very similar to meteorite material. This would indicate that much of it comes from the Asteroid Belt. But some particles seem different from anything found on Earth, on the Moon, or in meteorites. These particles may have come our way from the far corners of the universe. Some may have drifted our way on their own. Others may have been swept toward Earth by comets—those ghostly visitors of the solar system.

Comet Kohoutek gleams as it travels past Earth in 1973.

Comets: Ghostly Visitors

Many people say they've seen comets streaking across the sky. But that can't be so. When seen from Earth, comets do not appear to move rapidly.

An object streaking across the sky would likely be a meteor burning its way through the atmosphere. Or it could be a piece of old spacecraft falling back to Earth. When you see a comet, you can be sure it is outside Earth's atmosphere. It's so far out that it doesn't seem to move. If you could watch a comet for several hours you'd notice changes in its position against a background of stars. But you'd never see one streaking across the sky.

Comets come from the outer regions of the solar system. There was so much mystery in the past about where they came from that they were sometimes called the "ghostly visitors" of space.

Scientists now know that comets travel around

the Sun. Their orbits are far from circular. In fact, they are as elliptical as footballs! A typical comet travels in from the outer limits of the solar system, cuts through Earth's orbit, where it may be seen in the sky for several nights, then makes a sharp turn around the Sun and heads back toward the outer regions.

Out there, beyond the planets, the comet may swing around and start on the long voyage back toward Earth and the Sun. Or it may disappear in the outer regions.

Expected Visitors

A great many comets are known to scientists. Most were named for the astronomers who first saw them: Comet Halley, Comet Kohoutek, Comet Mumason. The path of each named comet is known. So are the dates of its expected visits.

Some comets are frequent visitors to Earth's neighborhood. Comet Encke has passed by Earth fifty times since it was first seen in 1786. On the other hand, Comet Donati, which passed this way in 1858, won't be back until around the year 4000.

Another famous "ghostly visitor" is Comet Halley, which comes our way every seventy-five years. The English scientist Edmund Halley studied the comet during its 1682 visit, and he concluded that it was the same comet that had been seen in 1532 and 1607. During some of its expected visits, Hal-

The great tail of Halley's comet lights up the sky. All brightness is reflected sunlight. A comet gives off no light of its own.

ley's comet could barely be seen. But in 1910, it lit up the night sky for several weeks. In mid 1982, astronomers with powerful telescopes spotted the comet far out in space. It was on course and on time for its late 1985–early 1986 close encounter with Earth.

Comets that regularly visit Earth's neighborhood, whether once every five years or once every 5,000 years, are called *periodic comets*. There are, however, comets that seem to come this way just once. They're called *nonperiodic comets*. They sweep in from the edge of the solar system, then swing round the Sun, head back out . . . and are never seen again.

No Light of Their Own

Most comets can be seen only with the help of a telescope. But many are bright enough to light up the night sky. Some can even be seen in the daytime. But you can't count on a particular comet to always be bright. It may light up the sky for days on one visit. Yet on the next visit, it may only be seen through a powerful telescope.

Comet Kohoutek was expected to be brilliant during its 1973–1974 voyage past Earth. It wasn't! Most people were unable to see it without the help of a telescope.

Unlike meteors, comets do not give off light of their own. When you see a comet, you're seeing sunlight bouncing off the comet. The brightness of a comet depends on its size, shape, and closeness to the Sun. But most of all the brightness depends on the way sunlight strikes the comet as it passes near Earth.

Ice, chunks of solid matter, and gases are what a comet is made of. Most of this material is contained in the comet's nucleus. Some scientists say the nucleus is like a big, dirty snowball.

In most comets, the nucleus is surrounded by a cloud of gas. This is called the *coma*. The coma may be many times larger than the nucleus.

Together, the nucleus and the coma make up one basic part of a comet, the head. The other basic part of a comet is the tail. The tail is a mass of dust particles, ice specks, and gases streaming

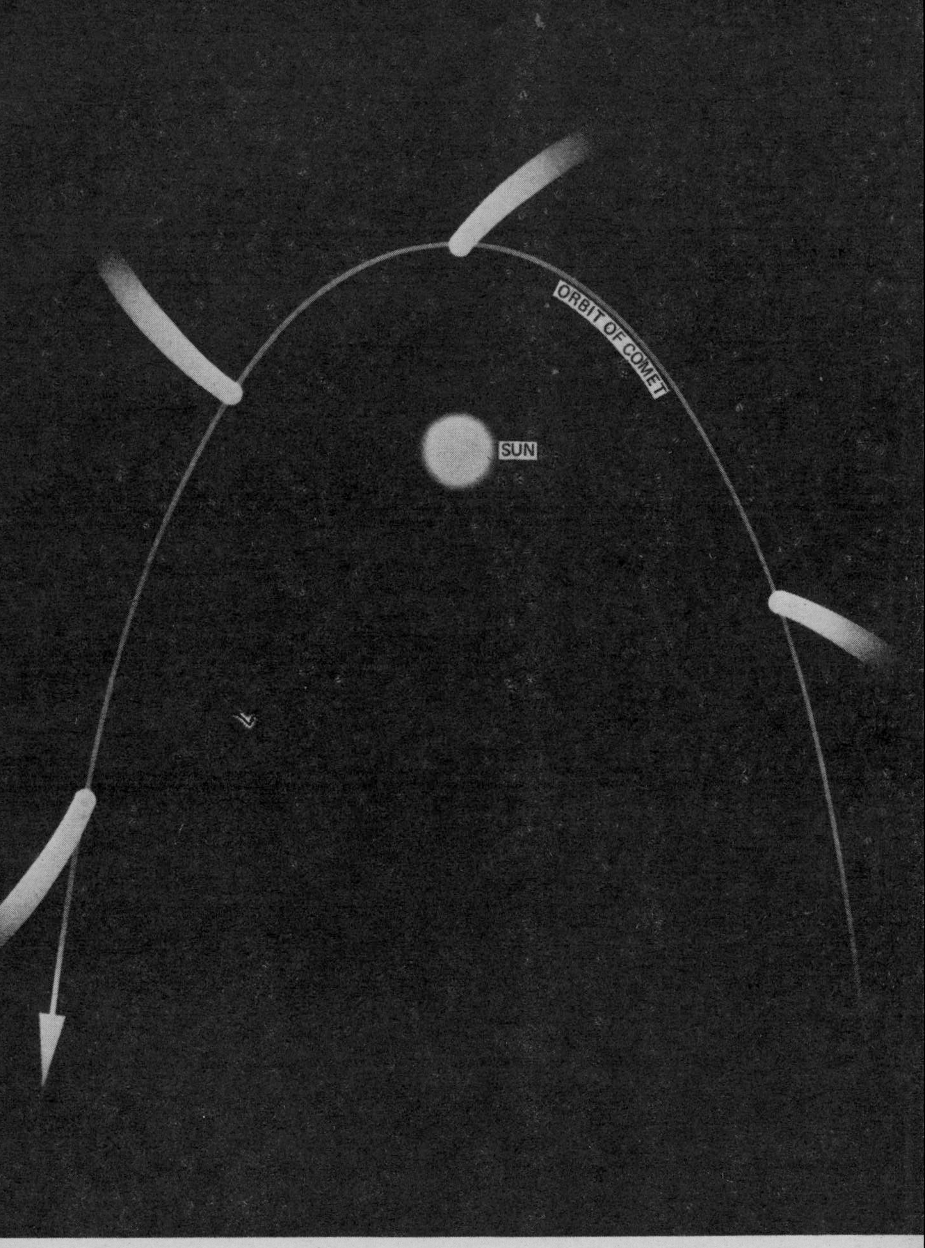

As a comet travels around the sun, its tail is blown outward by the solar wind.

out from the head.

The tails of some comets are huge. The tail of the Great Comet of 1843 was estimated to be 200 million miles long. Scientists figure that when a comet's tail is that long, the nucleus must be losing matter at a rapid rate. A few trips through the heat of the Sun could be the end of such a comet. And that may be why the Great Comet of 1843 has never reappeared.

Death of a Comet

Some comets passing Earth have had double, even triple, tails. But such unusual tails may be signs of trouble.

In 1826, an Austrian nobleman, Baron Wilhelm von Biela, identified and named Comet Biela. But when he wrote about it, several astronomers realized that they'd seen the comet before. They calculated that it passed by Earth every 6.7 years. From 1826 on, they eagerly looked forward to each visit of Biela.

On November 25, 1845, astronomers spotted Biela coming in toward Earth and the Sun. It was right on time, right on course. Throughout the rest of 1845 and on into 1846, they tracked Biela as it headed toward the Sun. Then, early in January, 1846, a strange thing happened. Biela flared brightly, brighter than before, and a few days later, the astronomers noticed that the comet had two tails. Some time later, the two tails split apart. Biela had become two comets!

For a time, the two comets drifted side by side. Then, for a brief period, another tail appeared that seemed to link the two comets. When that third tail vanished, the two comets drifted apart. They were last seen, near the end of February, 1846, traveling far apart toward the edge of the solar system. Astronomers wondered: Would the two comets come back on the predicted dates for the return of Biela? 1852, 1859, 1866, 1872, 1877–1878, 1885, etc.

Late in the fall of 1852, the two comets did reappear. They were hard to see, even through a powerful telescope, but they reappeared and they remained in view for just over a month. After that, they were never seen again.

But a strange thing happened on November 27, 1877. A great meteor shower lit up the sky that night. For over six hours, shooting stars put on a wondrous show. Astronomers say that over 160,000 chunks of matter plunged into Earth's atmosphere that night.

Did the great meteor shower of November 27, 1877, mark the final breakup of Comet Biela?

Many astronomers think so! They say that when we see a comet, it is on its death trip. That trip may take thousands of years. Or it may last only a few months. According to this theory, comets are at home near the edge of the solar system.

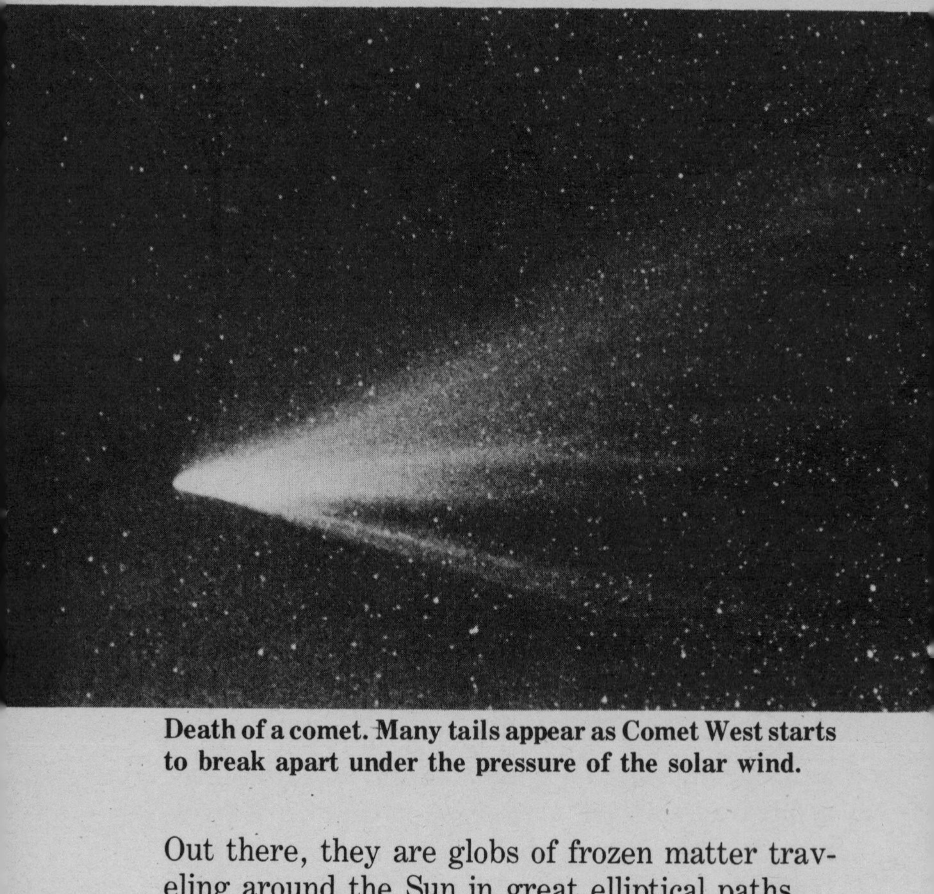

Death of a comet. Many tails appear as Comet West starts to break apart under the pressure of the solar wind.

Out there, they are globs of frozen matter traveling around the Sun in great elliptical paths.

French scientist Joseph Louis Lagrange (1736–1813) said that comets are masses of stardust from deep space. These stardust masses are trapped near the edge of the solar system. Every once in a while, one of these masses is knocked out of its orbit by some force and sent plunging toward the Sun. When this mass is seen from Earth, we call it a comet.

From the Edge of the Solar System

Though Lagrange made his suggestion almost 200 years ago, many astronomers still accept it. Others disagree; they say that comets are made of leftover material from the solar system. Both groups agree, however, that comets are at home near the edge of the solar system . . . unless they are disturbed. When a comet is disturbed, it will swing in toward the Sun. And that's when we get a chance to see it.

A comet may travel in toward the Sun and back out again hundreds of times. But all that time, the comet is falling apart. Energy and particles shooting out from the Sun bite into the comet's frozen nucleus, sending matter streaming out to form a tail.

A comet's nucleus may wear down slowly over a long period of time. Or it may suddenly break apart. Astronomers saw and photographed the breakup of a comet in March, 1976. The comet was named West, after the astronomer who first saw it coming in toward Earth five months earlier.

Comet West passed close to the Sun on February 25, 1976. Dozens of astronomers watched it glowing brilliantly as it headed away from the Sun. Then, over several days in early March, the comet's nucleus broke into pieces. Soon the pieces vanished from view. Some may have continued outward, too small to be seen. Others may have fallen into the great mass of the Sun. Pieces of Comet West may even have fallen to Earth.

A Comet That Came to Earth?

A number of scientists believe that comets have fallen to Earth at various times in the past. They say that some of the gases in Earth's atmosphere were brought here by comets millions of years ago. Other scientists question that idea. But they all agree that a comet could collide with Earth.

Several scientists now believe that a comet, or a piece of a comet, collided with Earth on June 30, 1908.

Early in the morning of that day, a bright flash lit up the sky over central Siberia. A tremendous explosion shattered the stillness of the forest near a place called Tunguska. Thousands of trees in the area were flattened. Windows were shattered nearly one hundred miles away.

At the time, it was thought that a huge meteorite had crashed to Earth. But when scientists finally went to the Tunguska area, they could find no trace of a meteorite. Neither did they find a hole where a meteorite might have plunged into the ground. They did find a scorched area, where all the flattened trees pointed out like the spokes of a wheel. From this evidence the scientists concluded that there had been a great explosion in the atmosphere above the forest.

But what could have caused such a huge explosion?

Over the years, there have been many suggestions as to the cause of the Tunguska explosion. Some people said that a spaceship from another planet blew up while trying to land there. Others suggested that the Imperial Russian Army was testing secret weapons in the forest. Still others said that a strange form of matter from space may have exploded when it met Earth matter.

Many scientists now believe that the explosion was caused by a small comet. The icy nucleus of such a comet would have heated fast as it sped through Earth's atmosphere. As a result, the nucleus might have burst apart. Such an explosion in the atmosphere would have scorched a piece of the ground, and flattened trees over a large area. It could have turned the material of the comet into fine dust that would have been scattered far and wide by the wind.

On the TV program *Cosmos*, astronomer Carl Sagan said, "There seems to be only one explanation. . . . In 1908, a piece of a comet hit the Earth."

Earth, as seen from a spaceship near the Moon.

Earth:
The Space Traveler

We live on a spaceship hurtling through a stormy universe. That spaceship is planet Earth!

Spaceship Earth has a life-support system—atmosphere, water, soil, and plants—that is powered by energy from the Sun. There could be no life on Earth without the Sun's energy. But too much of that energy could wipe out all life on Earth.

Earth's Double Shield

Life on Earth is shielded in two ways: by the atmosphere and by Earth's magnetic field, also called the *magnetosphere*.

The atmosphere protects us, most of the time, from meteoroids, certain radiant energy, comets, and showers of stardust. The magnetic field protects life on Earth from harmful radiation from the Sun and the stars, and, most of all, from the effects of storms on the Sun.

Scientists don't really know why Earth has a magnetic field or how it is set up, but they do all agree that Earth is a giant magnet in space. And they're thankful for that fact.

The Restless Sun

All life on Earth depends on the energy output of the Sun. So life on Earth is surely affected by any changes in that output. Even a small change can trigger big changes in our weather conditions. But why does the energy output of the Sun keep changing?

Energy is produced on the Sun in the same way that it is produced in the explosion of a hydrogen bomb. The process in both cases is *nuclear fusion*.

Intense heat causes lighter atoms (such as hydrogen atoms) to fuse, or merge together, to form heavier atoms. As the lighter atoms fuse together, heat energy is given off. This causes more atoms to fuse. More heat is produced. And so on.

This process is happening all the time within the Sun—it's an on-going fire storm.

Though the fire storm never stops, it does rise and fall. For some reason, relatively cool areas develop on the fiery surface of the Sun. These relatively cool areas are called *sunspots*. Seen from Earth, they appear as dark spots on the surface of the Sun.

As a sunspot forms, it spreads out. As it spreads, it triggers an explosion of super-hot gases above the surface of the Sun. This is called a *solar flare.*

Sunspots seem to occur in eleven-year cycles. That is, they increase in number until they reach a high point once every eleven years. Then they taper off.

No one knows why sunspots come in eleven-year cycles. In fact, no one really knows what causes sunspots. But scientists do know that when sunspots form, the Sun gives off great bursts of energy that cause changes in weather, interfere with radio signals, and often trigger amazing light shows in the sky near the North and South Poles.

Northern Lights

When they watched bright lights dance in their night sky, people living in northern Canada used to say that the gods were at war and had set heaven on fire. Old stories told by the Norse people, who lived in Iceland, Norway, and Sweden, explained that the gods were building "bridges of fire" from Earth to heaven. The old Norse name for the mysterious lights in the northern sky was *Bifrost*, or "fiery bridge."

Scientists never accepted those explanations and some made the dangerous, difficult journey to the north to study the dancing lights.

Like a ghost gone wild, the Northern Lights—*aurora borealis*—swirl and dance above an Alaskan town.

French scientist Pierre Gassendi (1592–1655) said that the northern lights were caused in some way by the movement of tiny chunks of matter in the upper air.

Gassendi wasn't able to say where the tiny chunks of matter came from or how their movements turned on the northern lights. And he couldn't explain why the lights seemed to appear only in far-northern skies at certain times of the year.

Gassendi did, however, give us our present name

for this wondrous display. He called it the *aurora borealis*, "northern dawn."

Almost one hundred years after Gassendi's time, the Swedish scientist Anders Celsius (1701–1744) made a startling discovery. Celsius found that the display of northern lights had something to do with changes in the Earth's magnetic field.

Celsius spent a lot of time in northern Sweden studying the aurora borealis. One March evening he decided to map the position of the lights. As he worked with his magnetic compass, Celsius noticed that each time there was a flash of light in the sky, the needle of the compass bounced around.

Celsius checked this again and again. On all occasions, the same thing happened. Each time the lights flashed in the sky, the compass needle bounced around. Celsius deduced that the northern lights had something to do with changes in the Earth's magnetic field.

But what was the link?

Celsius couldn't answer this question. Neither could anyone else for a long time.

It wasn't until almost one hundred years later that the next big clue in the mystery of the northern lights turned up.

Southern Lights

Crews of whaling ships, sailing the icy waters

of the South Atlantic, reported that strange lights also appeared in the sky near the Antarctic Circle. Men who had sailed both the Arctic and Antarctic regions said that the lights in both places looked very much alike.

When scientists heard about this, they named the southern lights *aurora australis* (*australis* is a Latin word meaning *southern*) and they wondered whether the displays of northern and southern lights were related. Could some single happening be triggering the mysterious lights at the opposite ends of Earth?

Those questions were partly answered in 1859 by the British astronomer Richard Carrington (1826–1875), as a result of his observations of the Sun. Carrington was studying the Sun through a special telescope when he spotted a fiery burst of energy from its surface. He called this a solar flare. He was the first astronomer to report such a flare of energy from the Sun.

A few hours after seeing the solar flare, Carrington noticed that the needles of his compasses were bouncing around. Those were signs that Earth's magnetic field was being disturbed. Carrington wondered whether the magnetic disturbance was somehow linked to the solar flare.

Other scientists asked: Could both events be related to the appearance of northern and southern lights?

Carrington wasn't sure. He went back to studying the Sun, while a number of other scientists started putting the pieces of the puzzle together. They found out that the aurora borealis and the aurora australis took place at the same time. They also found that Earth's magnetic field was disturbed at the time of the appearance of the lights. And what's more, they found that a few hours before each appearance a solar flare had been seen.

Putting it all together, the scientists felt sure that the solar flares were causing the auroras. But they didn't really know how this was happening.

At the time, scientists knew that the Sun bombards Earth with tiny chunks of matter and energy. They also knew that most of this radiation doesn't reach the surface. It's bounced away by Earth's magnetic field. So the scientists figured that when there's an extra burst of energy from the Sun—like a solar flare—there is extra pressure on Earth's magnetic field.

That would explain why Earth's magnetic field is disturbed by solar flares. But how would this cause dancing lights in the sky?

Norwegian scientist Olav Kristian Birkeland (1867–1917) set up an experiment to answer that question. He put a metal ball in a vacuum chamber—a box without air—and he caused the ball to spin. Then he set up a magnetic field around the spinning ball. Birkeland bombared the spinning ball with electrons—charged pieces of atoms.

RESTRICTED
AREA

He noticed two things.

Some of the electrons were bounced away by the magnetic field. Others moved toward the ball's magnetic poles. This caused a faint glow of light around both poles.

From this and other experiments, scientists figured out that the Sun's energy turns on Earth's northern and southern lights.

In recent years, scientists have stepped up their studies of the aurora borealis and the aurora australis. They hope to increase human knowledge of the polar lights and of Earth's magnetic field. But most of all they hope to gain more information about the Sun's energy system.

Exploring the Sun . . . on Earth

During the 1980's, the National Research Council of Canada launched small rockets from Canada's far north regions every time auroras were seen. As the rockets soared among the dancing lights in the northern sky, they made magnetic measurements.

On the basis of these and other measurements, scientists have been able to figure out the shape

Rockets launched into the northern sky, while the *aurora borealis* appears, measure changes in the Earth's magnetosphere.

of Earth's magnetic field. In terms of size and shape, scientists prefer to call the magnetic field the magnetosphere.

The magnetosphere is like a huge invisible cage surrounding and protecting Earth. This cage is formed by magnetic lines of force curving out from one of Earth's magnetic poles, and curving in at the other.

If the magnetosphere could be seen from way out in space, it would look like a teardrop about thirty times the size of Earth. The short rounded end of this teardrop always faces the Sun. That's where the solar wind presses against the magnetosphere. On the side away from the Sun, Earth's night side, the magnetosphere trails off into space.

The magnetosphere protects Earth from the fury of solar storms. But there are two holes in this protective shield. One is at the north magnetic pole. The other is at the south magnetic pole. In both places, particles from the stormy Sun slip into our atmosphere and light up the sky.

Over the years, people on Earth have kept written records of unusual auroras. From these records, scientists have been able to trace the recent history of the Sun. They have plotted stormy periods and quiet periods on the Sun's surface.

There appears to be a pattern to the Sun's activity. Every eleven years, there is a high point in solar flare activity. A great many flares may be seen over a period of some months. Then the flare activity tapers off.

This eleven-year cycle of solar flare activity is like the Sun's pulse or heart beat. Scientists don't understand why there is such a pattern to solar flare activity. But they know that it has been going on for a very long time.

Every once in a while, however, there's a burst of solar flare activity that's out of season. It's not part of the regular eleven-year pattern.

What could cause such out-of-season solar storms? A few scientists say that these out-of-season storms may be caused by disturbances of the Sun's magnetic field.

But what could disturb the Sun's magnetic field?

Some scientists say that a burst of energy from the explosion of a star, or a group of stars, would disturb the Sun's magnetic field. But the universe is so big that a burst of energy could take thousands, even millions, of years to reach the Sun from the point of explosion.

Life on this planet is shaped by the flow of energy from the Sun. And it seems that the energy from the Sun is influenced by flows of energy through the universe. Right now it's possible that life on Earth is being influenced by energy from a star explosion that occurred millions of years ago.

Brown-yellow clouds swirl around Venus, the planet nearest to Earth.

Venus: A Cloudy Mystery

Is there life on other planets?

In thinking about the question, scientists have usually looked toward Earth's neighboring planets—Venus and Mars. They seem most like Earth.

Venus, second planet from the Sun, is a lot like Earth in size and mass. Also like Earth it has a cloudy atmosphere. But there the likeness ends.

Photos of Earth taken from space, show a planet full of variety. Gray-green and brown land areas stand out against broad stretches of blue ocean. Over all, white clouds swirl and drift on the wind and leave shadow patterns on the surface.

There's nothing like that on Venus. Whether viewed from Earth or photographed from space, Venus shows no features at all. It looks like a bright, giant, Ping-Pong ball. That's because the planet is wrapped in thick clouds.

The United States spacecraft *Mariner 10* photographed Venus in 1974. Some of the photos were taken from as close as 5,000 miles. But all they showed were unbroken brownish-yellow clouds swirling around the planet. No wonder people call Venus a "cloudy mystery."

Scientists say that Venus has an atmosphere ninety times heavier than that of Earth. A person standing on the surface of Venus would feel the same pressure as if he or she were 3,000 feet beneath the sea.

Bad as this crushing pressure is, the worst thing about Venus, however, may be the heat. Scientists estimate that the surface temperature of Venus is around 900°F. That's hotter than most ovens. But that's not all. The hot, crushing atmosphere is made up mostly of stifling carbon-dioxide gas with clouds of acid droplets drifting in it.

It's very unlikely that anything could live in Venus' thick, hot, dense, poisonous atmosphere. Even robots designed to withstand great heat and pressure have trouble surviving in the place.

Robot Visitors

Many unmanned spacecraft have been sent from Earth to probe the mysteries of Venus. Soviet scientists have sent at least a dozen robot landing craft. The Soviets call their craft Venera. Six of these Veneras made it to the cloudy planet's surface and survived long enough to send some information back to Earth.

On October 18, 1967, after several unsuccessful tries, *Venera 4* plunged into the dense, yellow clouds of Venus. About thirty miles above the planet's surface, a special parachute opened and *Venera 4* drifted slowly down. Instruments on the spacecraft measured the temperature, pressure, and chemical makeup of the atmosphere. And this information was sent back to Earth.

When the flow of information from *Venera 4* stopped, the temperature reading was 540°F. The last pressure reading was twenty times greater than Earth's sea-level atmosphere. So scientists figured that *Venera 4*'s instruments were crushed or cooked by Venus' terrible atmosphere before the craft could reach the surface.

Two more spacecraft were sent—*Venera 5* and *Venera 6*. They also went down by parachute. And they also stopped transmitting before they reached the surface of Venus.

At this point scientists wondered: Can anything survive on Venus?

Touchdown

Each failure taught the scientists certain lessons. Designs of the Venera spacecraft were improved. And late in 1970 came the first hint of success.

A model of the *Venera 9* spacecraft that reached the surface of Venus.

Venera 7 and *Venera 8* successfully reached the surface of Venus. Each craft transmitted for just a few minutes. Then there was silence. Not much useful information came from *Venera 7* and *Venera 8*. But they had shown the way.

The next breakthrough came in 1975. *Venera 9* and *Venera 10* safely reached the surface. The two spacecraft survived long enough to send back lots of information and two photo images.

The data and photos from *Venera 9* and *Venera 10* showed the surface of Venus to be hot, dry, and dusty. The lower atmosphere was found to be hot, crushing, and poisonous.

This was backed up by information from *Venera 11* and *Venera 12* in 1978.

During 1978–1979, the United States spacecraft Pioneer went into orbit around Venus. Four small probing craft were sent toward the surface. Two of them reached the surface intact, and they survived long enough to send back information.

The Pioneer probes backed up the findings of the Venera craft, and provided one surprise. The United States probes revealed that there were tiny amounts of water vapor in Venus' lower atmosphere.

Lost Oceans?

Most of what we now know about Venus comes from the successful *Venera 13* and *Venera 14* missions of 1982. On March 1 of that year, *Venera 13* landed on a hilly area of Venus. Four days later, *Venera 14* landed in a lowland area. Both spacecraft sent information to Earth for more than two hours. That marked a record for survival on Venus.

Each craft sent back picture images of its land-

Using information from several space missions, an artist drew this concept of the mountains of Venus.

ing site and information about the surface and atmosphere there. And each showed a different picture of Venus.

According to Soviet scientists, *Venera 13* landed in an area of weathered foothills. "One can see small potholes covered with hillside waste," they said.

Venera 13 provided eight color pictures of the area. Tass, the Soviet news agency, said the pictures showed "Sharp rocks semicovered with fine dust and sand. . . . The rock is mostly brownish." One scientist said that a cloud of dust was kicked up as *Venera 13* landed.

The landing of *Venera 14* was different. No cloud of dust was produced. And photo images from the spacecraft showed layers of rock with some coarse soil. Pieces of the layered rock seemed broken, showing layers of different colors—shades of gray and brown, with a touch of blue.

From information sent back by *Venera 13* and *Venera 14*, scientists concluded that the surface of Venus was very hot and very dry. Most of it was fairly flat and smooth. But at least three mountain areas rise out of the smooth, level plain. And some of these mountains are active volcanoes.

Some scientists say that the smooth, level plain is like a dry sea floor. And they say the mountain areas are like large islands rising out of the dry sea.

This raises a question: Could there once have been oceans on Venus?

Dr. Thomas M. Donahue of the University of Michigan thinks it's possible. Since Venus is closer to the Sun, it gets twice as much solar energy as Earth does. If Venus once had oceans, Dr. Donahue argues, all the solar energy might have turned most of the water into steam. Then, with so much water vapor in the atmosphere, a greenhouse effect would occur.

With a greenhouse effect, solar energy would continue to come into the atmosphere. But much of the heat in that energy would be trapped in the thick, cloudy atmosphere. This would cause the atmosphere to get warmer and warmer.

If a number of volcanoes were to erupt, they would speed up the process. That's because the volcanoes would add large amounts of dust, carbon dioxide, and other gases to the atmosphere. This would thicken the atmosphere and trap more heat.

In time, enough heat would be trapped in the atmosphere to turn every drop of water on Venus into vapor. But it wouldn't stop there. As the heat continued to increase, the water vapor would break up into hydrogen and oxygen gases. Since it's very light, the hydrogen would escape into space. And the oxygen would react with water in the rocks to form rust.

Is that what happened?

Dr. Donahue thinks it could have happened. He calls it a "runaway greenhouse effect."

Evidence turned up by some of the Venera spacecraft support the idea. But whether there was a runaway greenhouse effect or not, we now know that Venus is a terrible place for life as we know it.

But what about Earth's other neighbor? Since Mars is farther from the Sun than Earth, heat is not likely to be a problem there. Could there be life on the fourth planet from the Sun?

More than 1,500 pictures, taken by the *Mariner 9* spacecraft, were pieced together to make this portrait of Mars.

Mars:
Earth's Red Neighbor

Mars, the red planet, has fascinated astronomers for a very long time. Markings may be seen on the planet, even through a small telescope. This led astronomers in the past to say that Mars had seas, continents, and canals.

Canals???

Many people reasoned that if there were canals on Mars, there must also be intelligent creatures to build them. Fifty years ago, Mars was considered the most likely place outside Earth to have life.

Changing color patterns were seen on Mars. And they were viewed as proof of plant life on the planet. The changes in color were thought to be changes of the plants with the seasons.

Over the years, a number of scientists became convinced that there was no life on Mars. But they couldn't be sure, and so there was always the hope that some form of life would be found there when space scientists explored the place.

Success and Disappointment

During the 1970's, United States space scientists explored Mars. Unmanned Mariner spacecraft flew by Mars and took some great pictures. Viking spacecraft probed, prodded, and analyzed the soil of Mars. And also took some great pictures.

The exploration of Mars has been a great success. It has also been a great disappointment for many people.

Why?

Pictures from the Mariner and Viking spacecraft proved that there are no oceans, continents, or canals on Mars. They also showed that it's very unlikely that there are intelligent beings on the red planet. The great success of the unmanned exploration of Mars killed a dream—the dream of intelligent, extraterrestrial beings in a neighboring world.

Though the Mariner and Viking programs killed a dream, they also opened up a whole new world of surprises. Photos from Mariner and Viking spacecraft showed Earth people a wonderful planet with mountains, canyons, and volcanoes mightier than anything on Earth.

A Moonlike Place?

At least ten years before any spacecraft came close to Mars, most astronomers had concluded that there were no seas or canals there. Astronomers even doubted that there were plants on Mars. But they weren't prepared for the shock of the first close-up picture of Mars.

In July 1965, *Mariner 4* passed by Mars and photographed a very small piece of the planet's surface. Twenty photos were beamed back to Earth. These first close-up photos showed an area pockmarked with craters. It looked like the surface of the Moon.

This discovery prompted many people to say that Mars was nothing more than a big, lifeless chunk of rock in space. *The New York Times* said the photos seem to rule out the chance that there is, or once was, life on Mars.

But *Mariner 4* wasn't the last word on the subject. Two more spacecraft, *Mariner 6* and *Mariner 7*, flew by Mars in 1969. They photographed different sections of the planet. The *Mariner 6* and *Mariner 7* photos were much sharper and clearer than the *Mariner 4* photos. And the *Mariner 6* and *Mariner 7* photos provided a much broader and more varied view of the red planet.

They showed cratered regions, areas that were fairly smooth, and areas that were rough and broken. As a result, space scientists concluded that the surface of Mars was much more varied than had been believed after the 1965 Mariner mission. The planet seemed full of surprises. And they concluded that it was not a moonlike place.

Down in a Dust Storm

Since Soviet scientists had successfully landed two spacecraft on Venus in 1970, they wanted to try to do the same thing on Mars a year later. One unmanned Soviet spacecraft was sent plunging into the thin atmosphere of Mars on November 27, 1971. Another followed on December 2, 1971. A great dust storm was raging on Mars at the time, and the first Soviet craft vanished in the dust storm. The other one seems to have made it to the surface. It sent out a messed-up radio signal for about twenty seconds, and then there was silence.

While the Soviet craft were plunging to their doom, a United States spacecraft arrived and started circling Mars.

The orbiting craft was *Mariner 9*. Under command from Earth, it waited for the dust to clear. When the dust cleared, *Mariner 9* started photographing the surface of Mars. It went on photographing the planet for several years, until it had pictures of the entire surface of Mars.

Mariner 9 photos of Mars provided several surprises. They showed a volcanic mountain, Mons Olympus, that was far bigger than any volcano

An artist's drawing of a Viking spacecraft hovering over the rocky surface of Mars.

on Earth. They also revealed a canyon many times longer, wider, and deeper than the Grand Canyon.

Mariner 9 photos also showed patterns of side-by-side cracks, shifting sand dunes, polar ice caps, and recent lava flows. What appeared to be a dried-up riverbed showed up on a few photos. That got scientists excited. It hinted that there may once have been flowing water on the surface. And where there's water, there's the possibility of life.

Life on Mars?

From the *Mariner 9* photos and other studies, most scientists concluded that there were no large animals or plants on Mars. But they didn't rule out the possibility of germs and microbes in the Martian soil.

Was there microscopic life on Mars? How could people on Earth ever answer that question?

NASA set up the Viking Mars exploration program to answer that and other questions. The objective of the program was to put unmanned spacecraft in orbit around Mars. Then robot laboratories would go down from those spacecraft to the surface of Mars. On the surface, the robot craft would analyze and photograph the soil, rocks, and atmosphere of the red planet.

During the summer of 1976, Americans were celebrating the 200th birthday of the United States. This celebration was mostly on Earth, but part of it took place in space. During that summer, two American spaceships landed on Mars. They were the *Viking 1* and *Viking 2* robot landing craft.

Viking 1 made a smooth touchdown on July 20. *Viking 2* landed safely several weeks later.

While they were landing, instruments on both craft measured the atmosphere. They showed that Mars' thin atmosphere was made up of carbon dioxide with small amounts of nitrogen and argon.

After landing, cameras on both spacecraft started photographing their surroundings. The

Robot arm from *Viking 2* picks up a sample of Martian soil.

resulting television images were flashed back to Earth.

The two Vikings landed far apart. But the pictures they sent back were very similar. Both sets of pictures showed rolling deserts spotted with rocks. At both landing sites, the sandy soil was reddish brown. Red, brown, and yellow rocks were scattered here and there. And above all this, was an orange-yellow sky.

In addition to cameras and little weather stations, both spacecraft carried instruments to test the Martian soil for signs of life.

None of the tests turned up any definite signs of life. But one test did give the scientists something to think about.

In that test, a sample of Martian soil was put in a special box containing water vapor from Earth. If there were microbes in the Martian soil, they should slowly give off very small amounts of carbon dioxide. That's what happens on Earth.

But when the Martian soil came in contact with the water vapor, it gave off a sudden burst of gases.

Microbes on Earth do not react like that. Could there be some very unusual microbes in the soil of Mars? Or might that soil have a strange chemistry? The gases given off in the Martian soil included carbon dioxide, nitrogen, and small amounts of oxygen.

Most space scientists think that some unusual

chemistry was at work. All in all, the Viking experiments did not find proof of life on Mars. But they did not completely rule out the possibility of microscopic life there.

The unmanned space probes to our neighboring planets have shown that Venus is too hot, and Mars seems too cold for life as we know it. Many space scientists have shifted their interest to the outer limits of the solar system . . . and far, far beyond.

Saturn and its satellites were photographed from a distance of over 66 million miles by the Voyager spacecraft.

Jupiter and Saturn: Riddle of the Rings

Saturn—sixth planet from the Sun—is circled by bands of bright rings.

Jupiter—biggest of the outer planets—has a mysterious red spot.

Saturn's rings and Jupiter's Great Red Spot have been viewed through telescopes on Earth for over 300 years. And for as long, they have been a source of mystery and wonder.

People asked: Why does Saturn have rings? Why don't other planets have rings? What are the rings made of? What causes the Great Red Spot on Jupiter?

Scientists dreamed of the day when spaceships from Earth would take a close look at these outer planets.

And that day has come.

Four spaceships have been launched from Earth to the outer planets. They are still traveling far out in space. They are *Pioneer 10* and *Pioneer*

11, and *Voyager 1* and *Voyager 2*.

Pioneer 10 left Earth on March 2, 1972. *Pioneer 11* followed on April 5, 1973. They were the first spacecraft designed to travel past the outer planets of the solar system.

The two Voyager spacecraft were sent on a similar journey in the late summer of 1977. After their close encounters with Jupiter, both Voyager spacecraft moved on toward Saturn. *Voyager 1* passed by the great ringed planet in late 1980 and *Voyager 2* followed in mid 1981.

Jupiter and Saturn were found to be alike in some ways, and very different in other ways. Both planets are giants of the solar system. Both have internal sources of heat. Both have complex systems of rings and moons. And both have stormy atmospheres.

The Voyager pictures, however, showed that storms on Saturn are quite tame compared to those on Jupiter. Saturn's atmosphere is much less colorful than that of its sunward neighbor. And there is nothing like the Great Red Spot on Saturn's surface.

These space missions answered some old questions and raised some new ones. They also turned up a few big surprises.

Ring Surprises

One very big surprise was the discovery that

Saturn was not the only planet with rings. Rings were seen around Jupiter and Uranus. And several astronomers suspect that Neptune also has rings.

Looking at Saturn from Earth, astronomers thought the planet had four or five very wide rings. But pictures from the Voyager spacecraft showed that each wide ring is really a band of many narrow rings. There are actually thousands of rings around Saturn.

The rings of Jupiter turned out to be fewer, smaller, and much dimmer than the great sparkling rings of Saturn. So dim, in fact, that astronomers can't figure out from the photos just how many Jupiter rings there are.

The *Voyager 2* photos show a kind of double ring system—a brighter ring on the outside with a much fainter ring on the inside, which seems to stretch down to Jupiter's cloud cover. This inner ring might be made up of a group of faint rings.

Astronomers think the rings of Jupiter are made of very small particles of dust, ice, and gas. The particles seem to be much finer, fewer, and more spread out than the particles in the bright rings of Saturn.

The rings of Saturn proved to be tremendously exciting. *Voyager 1*'s cameras revealed that Saturn has thousands of rings, grouped into six broad bands with distant gaps in between. The rings are made up of chunks of rock and ice. Most of these chunks are tiny. But some are as big as small

Voyager photographs revealed that there are thousands of rings around Saturn, grouped in five or six wide bands.

moons. In fact, some *are* small moons.

Moon Surprises

Before the space missions, it was thought that Saturn had nine moons and that Jupiter had twelve. The space missions revealed that Saturn has at least twenty-one moons and that Jupiter has at least fifteen—four large moons and at least eleven small ones.

Each of Jupiter's large moons—Io, Europa, Ganymede, and Callisto—is about the size of a small planet. In fact, Callisto and Ganymede are bigger than the planet Mercury. And Io and Europa are nearly as big.

Voyager 1 passed close to Io and discovered that it was a place of intense volcanic activity. Great eruptions send fountains of hot sulfur and fiery gases squirting hundreds of miles above Io's rocky surface.

Voyager 2 passed close to Europa, the brightest of Jupiter's moons. Close-up pictures show a fairly smooth surface—no craters or mountains—but covered with cracks. Europa looks like a battered Ping-Pong ball. Some scientists suggest that Europa's rocky interior is covered with a thin coating of ice. If that is so, stresses could crack the ice and give the surface a cracked appearance. An ice coating would reflect great amounts of light, thus making Europa the brightest moon.

Jupiter and four of its moons—Callisto, Europa, Ganymede, and Io.

Callisto and Ganymede, Jupiter's largest moons, seem to be mixtures of ice and rock. Callisto's surface is pockmarked with craters, while Ganymede has some cratered areas and some smooth areas.

A few scientists say that Callisto is probably the oldest of Jupiter's moons, maybe even older than Jupiter.

How can a moon be older than its "parent" planet?

As a swirling mass of stardust started to form into the Jupiter system billions of years ago, Callisto may have been the first solid object to come out of it. And Jupiter may have been one of the last.

Saturn's Moons

The Voyager mission discovered a number of tiny moons near the edges of Saturn's rings. Astronomers call these tiny moons *shepherd moons* because they seem to herd Saturn's rings into distinct groups. The force of gravity of the shepherd moons seems to pull the rings together.

Some scientists think that the rings of Saturn were once moons that broke apart millions of years ago. They say some of the moon material broke into fine particles and formed the rings. Some remained in fairly large chunks—these they say, are the shepherd moons.

Other scientists don't agree with this idea. They think the rings contain the material for moons that never got a chance to form. They say the shepherd moons were once asteroids that were drawn in and held by Saturn's gravity.

Saturn's moons range in size from chunks of rock no more than fifty miles across to an object almost as big as the planet Mars. The object, called Titan, is the only moon in the solar system with a deep, dense atmosphere.

Because of its size and atmosphere, Titan seems more like a planet than a moon. Clouds float in Titan's thick atmosphere, and some form of rain may fall there. Titan is a cold, cold place, colder than any place on Earth.

The atmosphere of Titan is mostly methane gas. A number of scientists say that Earth may have had a similar atmosphere around a billion years ago. Early forms of life probably existed on our planet at the time. Does that mean there might be life on Titan?

It's very unlikely!

Instruments on *Voyager 1* measured a temperature of around -140°C on Titan's surface. Of course, it was a distant measurement. But most space scientists think it's close to being right. And they point out that life, as we know it, isn't likely to exist at that low temperature.

Just before leaving the area of Saturn in late 1981, *Voyager 2* turned up another mystery. It photographed the mysterious two-faced Iapetus.

Iapetus is one of Saturn's outer moons. It's much smaller than Titan and has a very special feature. It is half white and half black.

Scientists feel sure that the white half of Iapetus is an ice-covered area. But they're not at all sure why the other half is black.

Could the black material be volcanic rock that erupted from inside Iapetus? If this were the case, why would it cover only half the moon?

Could the black material have rained down on Iapetus from somewhere in space? Some scientists say it might have come from Phoebe, Saturn's outermost moon. After all, the dark side of Iapetus is the one closest to Phoebe.

The riddle of Iapetus was left unsolved as *Voyager 2* sped off through space for a future encounter with the planets Uranus and Neptune.

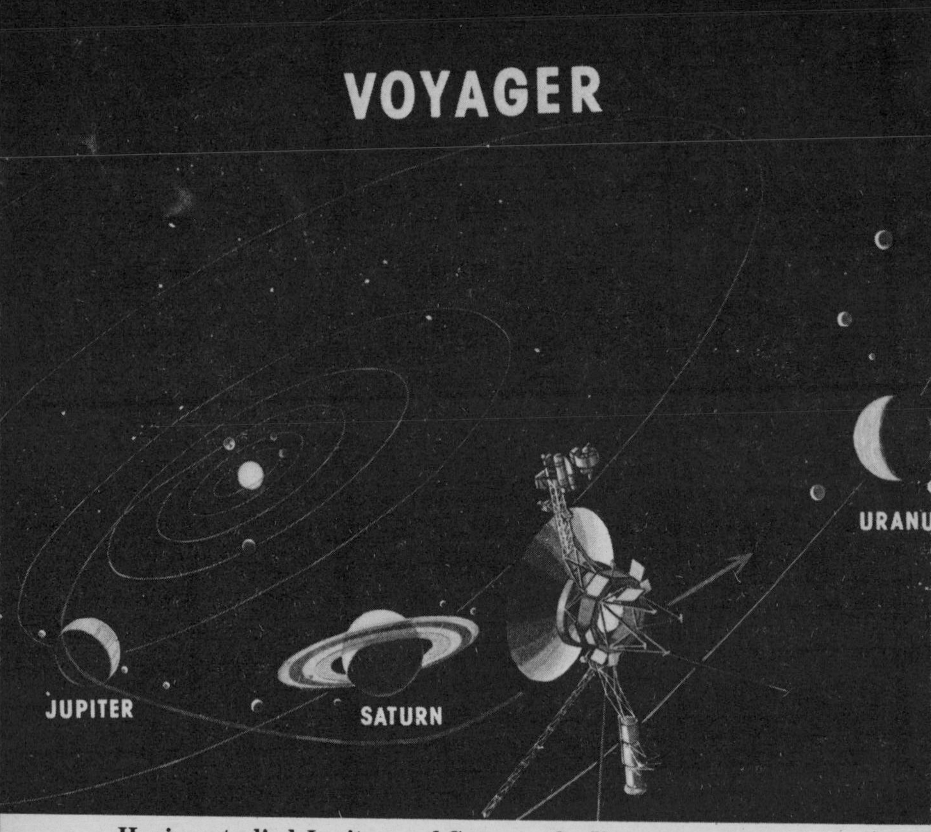

Having studied Jupiter and Saturn, the *Voyager 2* spacecraft is traveling on to Uranus (due 1986) and Neptune (due 1989).

To Uranus . . . and Beyond

Even through the most powerful telescopes on Earth, Uranus and Neptune are seen as remote, fuzzy objects. And very little was known about either planet until 1977.

Uranus and Neptune are almost the same size. They are smaller than Jupiter and Saturn. But they are giants compared to the four inner planets—Mercury, Venus, Mars, and Earth—of the solar system. Like Jupiter and Saturn, Uranus and Neptune are classed as frozen, gassy giants of the outer region of the solar system.

The Dark Rings of Uranus

In the mid-1970's, astronomers knew that Uranus would pass between Earth and a very bright star in 1977. They looked on this as a great chance to get a clear view of the distant planet.

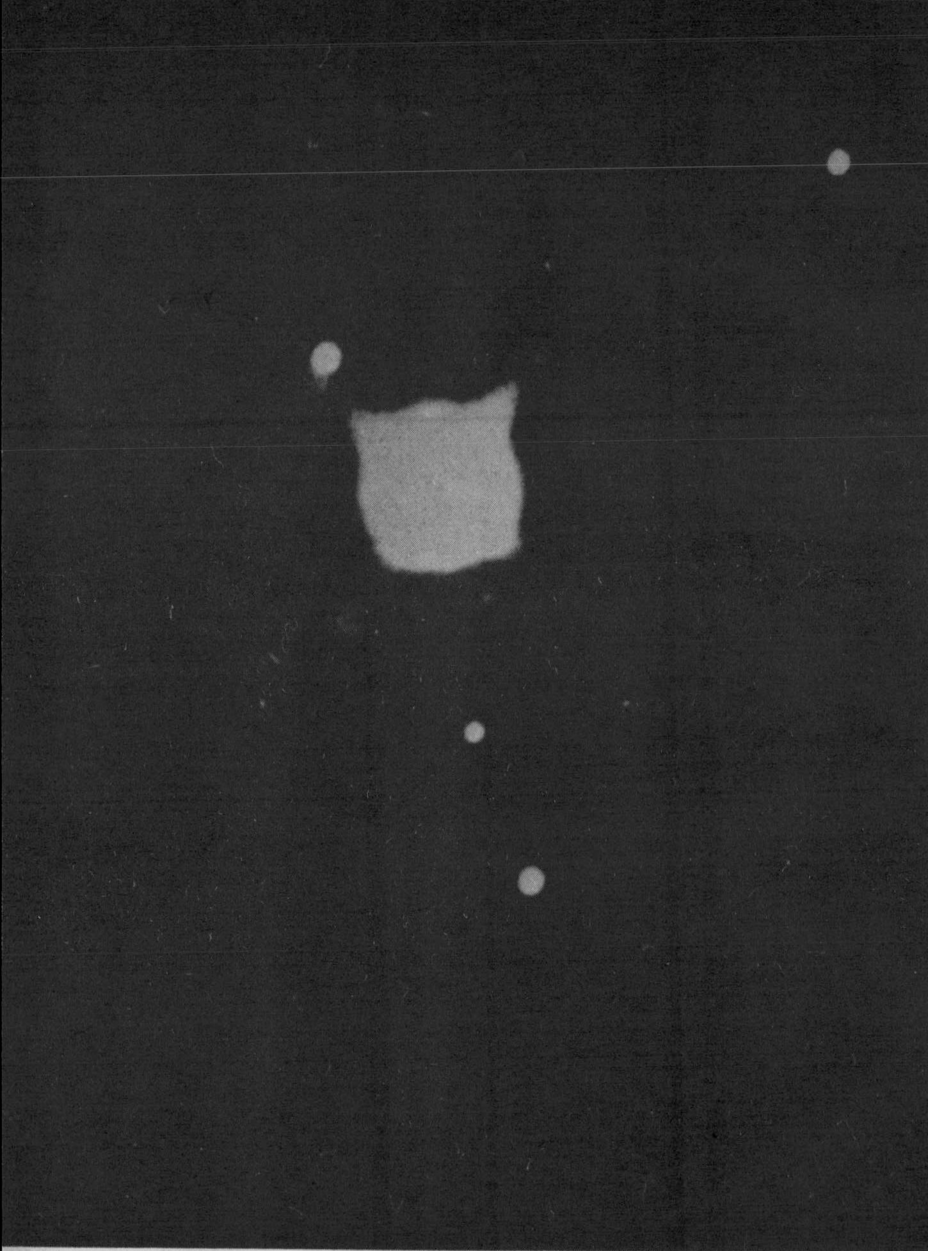

When viewed from Earth through the most powerful telescope, Uranus is still a dim, fuzzy object and its moons are mere dots.

As Uranus passed in front of the star, the astronomers would be able to measure its size and shape against the background of bright starlight. But there was one problem with this plan. They would have to photograph through Earth's atmosphere, which would dim the view. Dust, smoke, and water vapor in our atmosphere would tend to scatter and blur the starlight outlining Uranus.

What could be done about this?

NASA provided an answer. Their scientists turned a big jet plane into a high-flying observatory. They loaded it with a telescope, cameras, and other equipment.

When the time came to view Uranus, this high-flying observatory was cruising above seventy-five percent of Earth's atmosphere. The astronomers were able to get a clear view of Uranus.

An instrument was set up in the flying observatory to measure the length of time the star's light would be blocked as Uranus passed in front of it. With this measurement, astronomers would be able to calculate the width of Uranus.

As Uranus started to pass in front of the bright star, the star's light blinked on and off a few times. Then the light was completely blocked for a brief period as the bulk of Uranus passed in front of the star. Finally, as Uranus started to move away, the light blinked again.

What was causing the starlight to blink on and off?

A few scientists thought that the moons around Uranus were causing the blinking. Uranus has five known moons. But when their positions were checked, it turned out that none of them could have blocked the light.

After further study, space scientists discovered that the starlight blinked in a regular pattern as Uranus approached, and moved away from, in front of the star. The scientists then concluded that the starlight was blocked by a series of narrow rings around Uranus. Additional studies backed up this conclusion.

The rings of Uranus turned out to be very different from those of Saturn and Jupiter. The rings of Saturn and Jupiter are light and bright. Those of Uranus are quite dark.

Some scientists think the rings of Uranus are made up of chunks of black carbon. There may be some other rocks mixed in, but there are no signs of ice, which is what makes the rings of Saturn and Jupiter bright.

Uranus has five known moons. None is very big. There may also be a number of small shepherd moons in the narrow, dark rings of Uranus. In fact, the dark rings may be moons in the making.

Very little is known about the surface of Uranus. It appears to have a greenish atmosphere. And some pale clouds may float in it. Dark markings have been seen on Uranus. But astronomers aren't sure whether the markings are features of the surface or storm systems in the atmosphere.

Neptune and the Wrong-Way Moon

Neptune is slightly smaller in size than Uranus. No rings have yet been seen around the planet. But scientists wouldn't be surprised if rings were there.

The four giant planets of the solar system have several things in common. Each contains large amounts of frozen gases. Each has a cloudy atmosphere. Each has several moons. Three of those giant planets have been found to have rings.

Space scientists expect the Voyager spacecraft to find rings around Neptune, as well as some moons. Neptune is known to have two moons and there's evidence of a third one.

One of Neptune's known moons is like no other moon in the solar system. It's named Triton. And it's nearly as big as Saturn's Titan and Jupiter's Ganymede. That makes it one of the giant moons of the solar system.

However, unlike any of the other big moons in the solar system, mighty Triton is a wrong-way moon. Most moons spin in the same direction as their planet. Triton spins in the opposite direction.

There are other wrong-way moons in the solar system. But they are all very small. Many scientists consider that those small wrong-way moons are really asteroids that were drawn into orbit

The arrow points to lonely Chiron, an asteroid traveling around the Sun between the orbits of Saturn and Uranus. This photo led to the discovery of Chiron.

around certain planets. Except for Triton, no other large moon travels in a direction opposite to the rotation of its parent planet.

Why does Triton travel in the "wrong" direction?

Some scientists think that a great disturbance may have taken place in space near Neptune long, long ago. That disturbance could have sent some of Neptune's moons spinning off into space, and changed the rotation of Neptune. Or it could have changed the orbit of Triton.

If some moons were sent spinning away from Neptune, where are they now?

A few scientists say that one of the "missing moons" may be Chiron.

Chiron is an asteroid traveling around the Sun between the orbits of Saturn and Uranus. It was first discovered in 1977. And it appears to be the first known asteroid outside the Asteroid Belt.

Chiron is not a very big object. It's no more than a few hundred miles wide. But that's bigger than many of the moons around Saturn and Uranus. There are no signs of past disturbances in the moon systems of Saturn or Uranus. But there are signs of possible past disturbance among the moons of Neptune. So, though it's a long way from Neptune now, Chiron could be one of Neptune's "missing moons."

A few astronomers argue that two other "missing moons" of Neptune might be the planet Pluto and its moon, Charon.

Pluto: the Odd Planet

Most of the time, Pluto is the ninth planet from the Sun. But because Pluto's path around the Sun cuts through the path of Neptune, sometimes Pluto is the eighth planet from the Sun.

Pluto's existence was predicted long before the planet was seen. Astronomers noted wobbles in the orbits of Uranus and Neptune. They figured that these wobbles were being caused by the gravitational pull of a planet farther out in space.

As they searched for it, astronomers called the unknown planet, Planet X. They scanned the skies, and they scanned photos of the skies in their search for Planet X.

Then one day in 1930, astronomer Clyde Tombaugh spotted an unusual object on some sky photos. The object looked like a very small, distant planet. Tombaugh checked and double-checked. He talked about his findings with other astronomers. Finally, they concluded that the object was indeed a planet beyond the orbit of Neptune.

Planet X had been found. And a short time later it was named Pluto.

At first, astronomers thought that Pluto was about the size of Mars. Later studies forced them to conclude that Pluto is much smaller than Mars. It is smaller than Mercury. And it may even be smaller than Earth's Moon.

This prompted some astronomers to suggest that Pluto is not a planet at all. They say it may be an asteroid or a runaway moon.

The asteroid and runaway moon ideas got a setback in 1978. At that time it was discovered that Pluto has a moon of its own. This small moon was named Charon.

This discovery convinced some astronomers that

Pluto was indeed a planet. But others still argue that both Pluto and Charon could be asteroids. Or they could be runaway moons.

But if Pluto isn't a planet, does that mean Planet X is still out there waiting to be discovered?

Some space scientists think so!

A Tenth Planet?

Irregularities in the orbits of Uranus and Neptune suggest that there is a large object beyond Pluto. Data from *Pioneer 10* and *Pioneer 11* back up this suggestion.

NASA scientists say there may be a planet, about the size of Neptune, 5 billion miles beyond Pluto. But they also say that the mystery object might be a dark star 50 billion miles beyond Pluto.

This dark companion of the Sun could be a neutron star—an object that was once a big star but then collapsed. A star bigger than the Sun could collapse to become a neutron star smaller than Earth.

It's even possible that the object out there might be a black hole! That's a collapsed star that has become so dense that no light or any other form of energy can escape from it.

There are many double stars in the universe, and many dark companions to bright stars. So astronomers wouldn't be terribly surprised if the mystery object beyond Pluto turned out to be a dark star companion of our Sun.

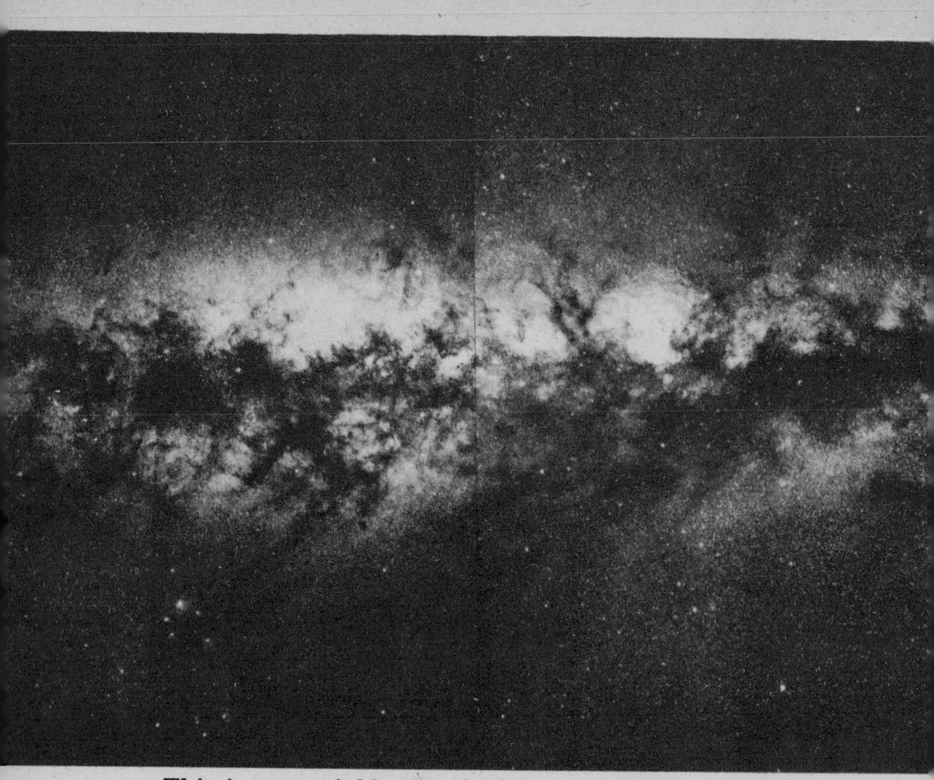

This is our neighborhood of stars, the Milky Way. Our Sun is a middle-sized, middle-aged, not-too-bright star in this galaxy.

Out of Stardust . . .

Our Sun is a star. It's a fairly ordinary star. It's not as big as some or as small as others; not as young or as old; not as hot or as cold.

There are billions of other stars like it in the universe. Some are "near" neighbors, less than a dozen light-years away. Others may be billions of light-years away.

Star Neighbors

Unless our Sun has a hidden dark star companion out beyond Pluto, its nearest star neighbor is Alpha Centauri.

Alpha Centauri is 4.3 light-years away. Since light travels 186,282 miles a second, the distance from the sun to Alpha Centauri works out to around 25 trillion miles.

That sounds like an enormous distance. But in in space, it's practically next door.

Without the use of a telescope, Alpha Centauri appears to be a single star. But astronomers have found it to be a system of three stars. The two larger stars in the system—Alpha Centauri A and Alpha Centauri B—revolve around each other. They are as far from one another as Saturn is from our Sun.

Alpha Centauri A, the brighter of the pair, gives off about the same amount of light as our Sun. Alpha Centauri B gives off about half that amount of light.

Many years ago, astronomers saw a very faint star near Alpha Centauri. They thought it was an independent star. Since they thought it was the closest one to the Sun, they called it Proxima Centauri.

Recently, a number of astronomers concluded that Proxima Centauri is not an independent star. They say it is actually part of the Alpha Centauri star system. Now they call it Alpha Centauri C.

The Brightest?

Although Alpha Centauri is our nearest star neighbor, it is not the brightest star in our sky. That honor goes to Sirius.

Sirius is about 8.6 light-years away. That's about twice the distance from Alpha Centauri to the Sun.

For a star so distant to shine so brightly in the sky, it must give off an enormous amount of light. It does! Sirius gives off about thirty times as much light as our Sun. There are a great many stars in the universe that give off more light, but they are much farther away.

Though it appears as a single point of light in the sky, Sirius is actually a double star. And the two parts of this double star system revolve around each other.

Each of the two stars in Sirius seems to be bigger than our Sun, and much hotter.

Compared to our Sun, Sirius is big and powerful. But compared to the second brightest star in the sky, Sirius is relatively small and cool.

That second brightest star is Canopus. And it is more than 100 light-years away. Canopus is many times bigger than our Sun. And it gives off

2,000 times more light.

The third brightest star in our sky is our close neighbor, Alpha Centauri. The fourth is Arcturus, 36 light-years away, and the fifth is Vega, which is 26 light-years from us.

Our near neighbors among the stars, in addition to Alpha Centauri and Sirius, are Barnard's Star, Wolf 359, and Lalande 21185. (Wolf and Lalande are the names of astronomers who discovered these stars. The numbers show these were the 359th and 21,185th stars they discovered.) Though they are relatively close to us, they are dim and difficult to see without a telescope.

Life Among the Stars?

Do other stars have systems of planets like our Sun? If so, could some of those be Earth-like places with intelligent life?

Some astronomers say that there may be billions of stars in the universe with planet systems. And the chances are that some of those countless planets may be Earth-like places with intelligent life. But we may never know.

Evidence that the bright star Vega may be circled by planets was turned up by an orbiting observatory in 1983. Special instruments on the observatory—the Infrared Astronomy Satellite—detected that Vega is surrounded by a cloud of solid material. Objects in the cloud seem to range

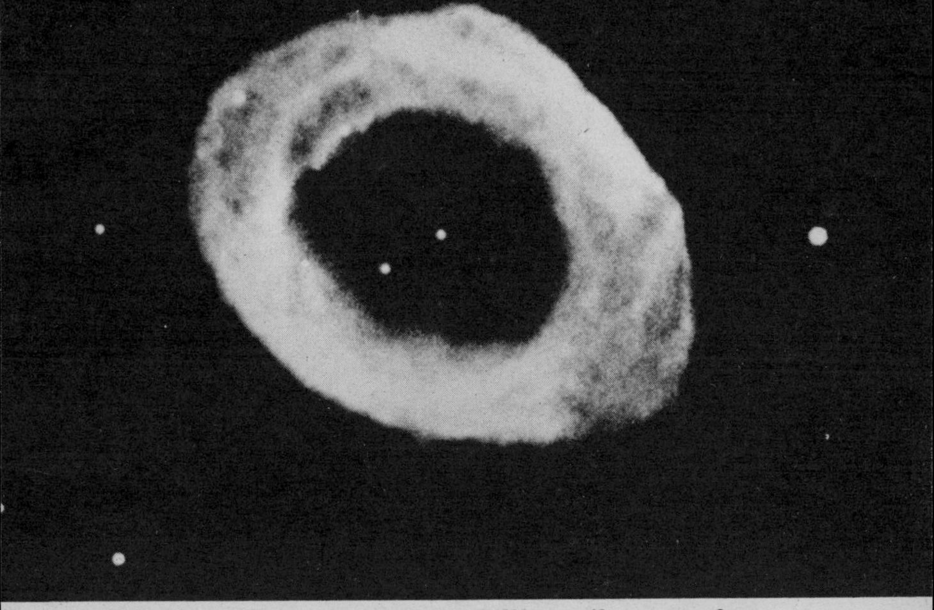

This ring nebula, about 15,000 billion miles away from Earth, contains masses of dust and gases out of which stars are formed.

in size from pebbles to planets. And several astronomers concluded that the cloud around Vega is a planet system being formed.

In addition to this direct evidence of objects circling Vega, there is indirect evidence that other stars are circled by planets. Several stars have been seen to wobble as they move through space. The most obvious is Barnard's Star. Astronomers say that this wobbling motion may be caused by the pull of large planets going around those stars. If this is true, then a great many stars in the universe have planet systems. And many of the planets may be like Earth.

There may be millions of other planets like Earth in the universe. And since they would be going through different stages of development, some might contain life forms. For most of its existence, Earth has been without life. Intelligent beings have been on Earth for only a tiny fraction of its existence.

Earth, and even our solar system, is just a tiny speck in space and time. Our Sun is part of a vast system of stars known as the Milky Way Galaxy. There are around 100 billion stars in this system. But that is just the beginning. Our galaxy is only one of several billion galaxies in the universe. And each one contains hundreds of billions of stars. That adds up to a mind-boggling number.

Lives of the Stars

In the vastness of the universe, everything is moving, everything is changing. We—our planet, our solar system, our galaxy—are part of this movement. We are part of this change.

Stars are constantly changing in size, shape, color, and brightness. In most cases, these changes take place gradually over millions of years. So they can hardly be noticed.

Every once in a while, however, a star will change rapidly. The period of rapid change may be a few years or just a few months. Such changes remind people on Earth that stars have lifespans.

Stars are born out of condensing clouds of stardust. They grow old. And they die!

Hundreds of years ago, astronomers first noticed that every once in a while a faint star would blaze brightly in the sky. For a short time this star would shine more brightly than any other star in the sky. Then it faded over a period of months or years. And in the end, it vanished from view.

The astronomer Tycho Brahe (1546–1601) noticed such a star change in 1572. That was before the invention of the telescope. He saw and described how the star suddenly appeared in the sky, and became brighter day by day.

For a time, this star, which was named Tycho's Star, became the brightest object in the sky except for the Sun and the Moon. Tycho's Star became brighter than Sirius. It became brighter than the planet Venus. Then it slowly faded from view.

Astronomers started calling such a star *nova*, from the Latin word for "new." They thought they were seeing the birth of a new star.

Novas and Supernovas

Hundreds of years later, when astronomers were

able to study the stars through powerful telescopes, they realized that a nova doesn't mark the beginning of a star. It marks the end of one.

A star is born out of a swirling cloud of stardust. Some event in space, such as a great explosion, may pack the dust into a tight mass. Then, as the particles of dust and gas are pulled together by the forces of gravity, small particles fuse together to form bigger ones. As that happens, heat energy is given off. The heat energy causes more and more particles to fuse together. More and more heat is given off. And the process continues. But it can't go on forever.

For a time—perhaps billions of years—a star will get hotter and hotter. It will change in color from blue-white to glowing pale yellow to bright yellow-orange. Then, as the smaller, lighter particles are gradually used up, the process slows down.

As the fusion process slows down, the star gets redder and redder. Then at some point the matter of the star starts to collapse inward. This may cause a brief surge of energy. The star may flare big and bright for a time. This is called the "red giant" stage. But it can't last.

Clouds of glowing dust and gases shoot out from the star. There's a sudden brief flare-up of energy—a kind of "last gasp." This is the nova stage.

The burnt-out shell of the star falls in on itself. For a time it may give off a white glow. This is often called the *white dwarf* stage.

The collapse doesn't stop there. The material of the star is packed together by the forces of gravity. At this point, a teaspoonful of star matter would weigh several tons. This is the *neutron star* stage.

Finally, a limit is reached as to how tight the matter of the star can be squeezed. At this point, the remains of the star are so dense and so small that it can't give off any light or other radiation. And it doesn't reflect light or other radiation. It's a *black hole*!

How can anyone know that such an object exists?

The only way a scientist can locate a black hole is by seeing the effects of its gravity. If some unseen object seems to be pulling on stars and stardust, that object would be a black hole.

Not every star dies slowly. Some very big, very hot stars go out with a bang. As such a star starts collapsing, tremendous amounts of energy are released. Then the star explodes . . . shooting great globs of glowing dust and gas into the darkness of space.

Astronomers call such a huge star explosion a *supernova*.

A number of supernovas have been seen within the Milky Way. And each year, astronomers see signs of supernovas in distant galaxies.

A supernova marks the violent death of a star or group of stars. It can also mark the birth of

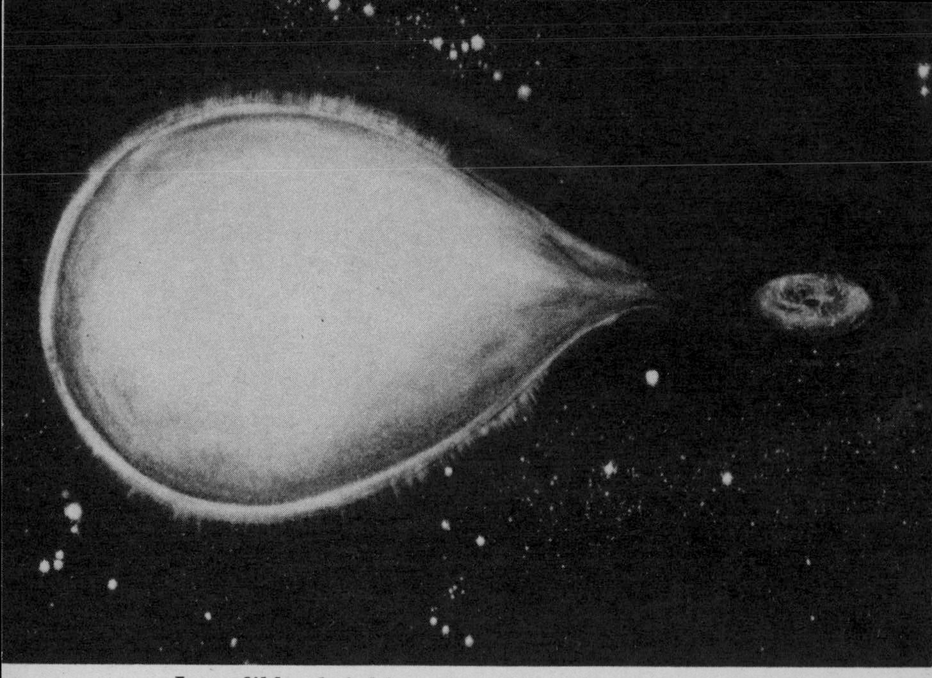

Incredible shrinking star. Black holes are believed capable of absorbing whole stars. This is an artist's conception of a black hole (right), an object so small and dense it can't give off light or other radiation.

another star. A group of scientists, meeting in New York recently, suggested that a supernova triggered the birth of our solar system billions of years ago. In their opinion, supernova explosions pushed a big cloud of stardust in on itself. As it squeezed together, the dust acted and interacted until finally it settled down into what is now our solar system.

Did the scientists have any evidence of this?

Yes! They showed some "invaders from space"—

small meteorites found at various places on Earth. Within the meteorites, the scientist found materials they believed were formed by supernova explosions billions of years ago.

The Andromeda Galaxy is the most distant object that can be seen from Earth without the help of a telescope.

Toward the Edge of Space and Time

Let's suppose we're in a super high-speed spaceship. We're traveling through the universe at the speed of light 186,282 miles per second.

From Earth it would take us 1.3 seconds to reach the Moon. It would take us about 2.5 minutes to reach Venus. And we would have to travel 6 minutes longer to reach the Sun.

Going in the other direction from the Sun, it would take us about 5.5 hours to get to the planet Pluto.

If we wanted to go to another star, our nearest star neighbor Alpha Centauri, it would take us 4.3 years.

Let's say we wanted to travel across our own star system. How long would that take us, traveling at the speed of light?

It would take about 100,000 years to travel across the widest area of the Milky Way Galaxy.

That's an awfully long time, just to go through our own starry neighborhood. But remember, the neighborhood contains around 125 billion stars.

Now let's crash out of the Milky Way by the shortest route, and visit some neighboring galaxies. How long would that take?

It would take 160,000 years to reach the Great Magellanic Cloud, which some astronomers say is our closest neighboring galaxy. Others don't call it a galaxy at all. They consider it an immense *nebula*. That's a cloud of stardust.

There are thousands, perhaps millions, of stars in the Magellanic Cloud. For that reason, a number of astronomers consider it a small, young galaxy.

There's another small galaxy out beyond the Magellanic Cloud. It's name is NGC 6822. But many astronomers don't take it seriously as a galaxy. The first major galaxy out from the Milky Way is M 31, or Andromeda.

We would have to travel 2.3 million years to reach Andromeda. But it would be worth the trip.

Andromeda is even bigger than the Milky Way. And millions of stars in that galaxy are likely to have planet systems similar to our own.

Though Andromeda is millions of light-years from Earth, it can be seen without the aid of a telescope. It is the most distant object in the universe that can be seen with the naked eye.

A Wealth of Galaxies

Astronomer Carl Sagan says there may be 100

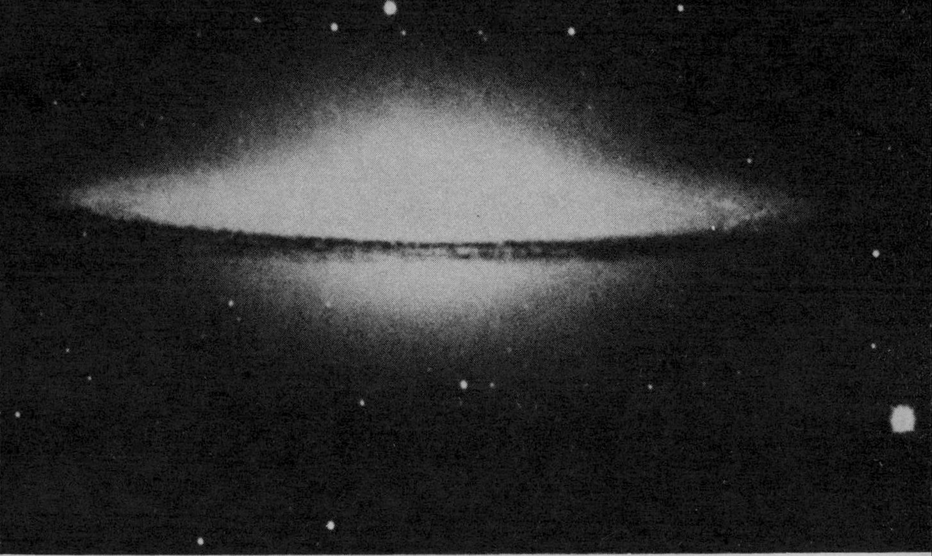

A spiral galaxy millions of light-years away. It is called the Sombrero Galaxy because its shape reminded astronomers of a sombrero.

billion galaxies in the universe. They come in a variety of shapes and sizes. Some are disk-shaped. Some are ball-shaped. And some are perfect spirals. At least a few are S-shaped. And several seem to have no particular shapes at all—they are uneven smudges of light in the darkness of the universe.

The largest galaxy known to astronomers is M 87. It holds, perhaps, two or three times as many stars as our Milky Way. Traveling from our solar system at the speed of light it would take 40 million years to reach M 87.

Beyond M 87, astronomers are watching two galaxies in collision. They are NGC 4038 and NGC 4039. In time they will merge into one blurred mass of stars and stardust.

At the speed of light, it would take us 50 million years to reach these colliding galaxies. That also means that when we view these galaxies from Earth, we are seeing them as they were 50 million years ago. That's how long it takes the light from those galaxies to reach us.

Seeing the Past

Every time we view an object in space we are looking into the past. When we look at objects in our solar system, we are gazing into the near past. We are seeing conditions as they were a few minutes or hours ago. But when we search out among the galaxies, we are seeing events that took place millions of years ago.

As astronomers watch the collision of galaxies NGC 4038 and NGC 4039 they are seeing an event that took place 50 million years ago. They have no way of knowing what's going on out there right now.

Right now, the two colliding galaxies may be exploding in a giant supernova. But people on Earth won't know about it for another 50 million years.

Radiant energy from such an explosion could affect life on Earth. But it would take 50 million years for radiant energy from that explosion to reach us.

The Outer Limit

As we look out into deep space, we are looking back into time. The more distant an object is from us, the older it is.

That brings up a tough question: What are the most distant and, therefore, the oldest objects we can see?

Most astronomers would say *quasars*.

These are mysterious sources of intense radiation in deep space. They were first discovered in 1963, when astronomers picked up very strong radio signals from way out in space. Later, some distant, dim objects were pinpointed as the source of the mysterious radio signals. Astronomers didn't want to call these distant objects stars. So they called them quasi-stellar (starlike) radio sources. In time, this was shortened to quasars.

After studying quasars for some time, astronomers concluded that they may be the most powerful objects in the universe. Quasars send out

Mysterious quasars near the outer limit of the known universe are estimated to be between 7 billion and 13 billion light-years away.

more radiant energy than stars, galaxies, novas, or supernovas. Astronomers also concluded that quasars are the most distant objects in the universe. They are estimated to be between 7 billion and 13 billion light-years away. That's out at the edge of the known universe.

But what exactly are quasars?

No one is sure. Some astronomers say they are distant galaxies going through violent changes. Thousands of stars may be colliding and exploding within such a galaxy.

If quasars are the most distant objects in the known universe, that means they are also the oldest objects in the universe. But when astronomers look at quasars, perhaps they are seeing the youngest objects in the universe.

How can that be?

A quasar 13 billion light years away may be the oldest object in the universe right now. But the light from that quasar took 13 billion years to reach us. So when an astronomer looks at the quasar he is not seeing it as it is now. He is seeing it as it was 13 billion years ago.

Some astronomers say that's going back beyond the age of our solar system—back almost to the beginning of the universe.

When we study the most distant quasars, maybe we are picking up signals from the edge of space and time. Maybe we are picking up signals from the beginning of time.

Index

**indicates photograph*